GO FACTS TRANSPORT

Trains

Trains

© Blake Publishing 2003
Additional material © A & C Black Publishers Ltd 2005

First published 2003 in Australia by Blake Education Pty Ltd

This edition published 2005 in the United Kingdom by
A & C Black Publishers Ltd, 37 Soho Square, London W1D 3QZ
www.acblack.com

ISBN-10: 0-7136-7286-2
ISBN-13: 978-0-7136-7286-2

A CIP record for this book is available from the British Library.

Written by Ian Rohr
Design and layout by The Modern Art Production Group
Photos by Photodisc, Brand X, Corel, Corbis, Image State, Comstock,
Digital Stock and Eyewire.

UK series consultant: Julie Garnett

Printed in China by WKT Company Ltd.

A & C Black uses paper produced with elemental chlorine-free pulp,
harvested from managed sustainable forests.

Contents

What Is a Train?

A train is a line of carriages. An engine pulls them along metal tracks.

Trains can be powered by coal, electricity or diesel fuel. Since trains run on **rails**, they can travel in all kinds of weather.

Trains are used around the world to move people and **goods**. Some trains travel short distances and others travel thousands of miles.

Commuter train

Carriage

Engine

Metal tracks

Old Trains

The first trains were pulled along by steam engines.

Steam engines burn coal. The burning coal heats water to make steam. The steam makes the wheels turn.

In the 1800s steam trains were a quick and cheap way to travel. People could travel for fun as well as for work.

Engineer

6

Today, most steam trains are for tourists.

FIRST!
The first steam-powered train was invented in 1829 by George Stephenson in England. It was called the *Rocket*.

Steam engines can be noisy and smoky.

60532

New Trains

Today, most trains have diesel or electric engines.

The new engines are quieter and cleaner than coal-powered steam engines. Diesel trains are often used in the country. Many electric trains run in cities.

Paris metro train

Some electric trains can travel very fast. They are called high-speed trains. The bullet trains in Japan can travel three times faster than a car.

Monorail trains only travel short distances.

High-speed trains get their power from overhead, electrical wires.

GO FACT!

DID YOU KNOW?
High-speed trains of the future will "float" along tracks using electromagnets.

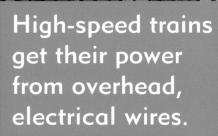

9

Peak Hour

People use trains to get to and from work. These trains are called commuter trains.

Commuter trains are busiest in the morning and in the late afternoon. These busy times are called peak hours.

Commuter trains began travelling underground 140 years ago. Now, many big cities have an underground train system.

Commuters

Some people take trains instead of driving to work.

Young people use trains to get to places.

Commuter trains travel above ground and underground.

GO FACT!

MOST!

New York City has the most subway stations with 468.

11

Long Trips

Some passenger trains travel long distances.

Long-distance trains can travel thousands of miles. People who take long trips, sleep and eat on the train.

Long-distance trains have special cars. Passengers sleep in a car called a sleeper. They eat their meals in the dining car.

Train traveller

Train ticket

Passengers eat meals in the dining car.

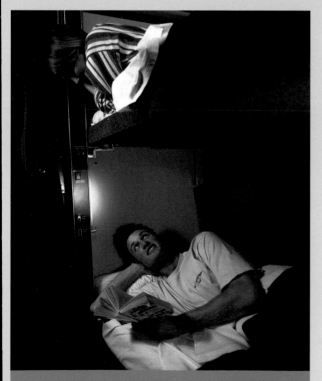

Bunk beds are common in sleepers.

Long-distance trains leave from large, busy stations.

Moving Goods

Freight trains move goods around the country.

Freight trains carry many different kinds of goods, such as coal, cars or cattle. Heavy freight trains travel more slowly than passenger trains.

Freight trains also take goods to **ports**. The goods are then put on ships and **exported** all over the world.

Freight train

Railway tracks take freight trains close to ports.

Coal is often moved by freight trains.

GO FACT!

LONGEST!

The longest freight train had 660 carriages and was pulled by 16 locomotive engines.

Freight trains can be over two miles long.

Glossary

commuter	a person who travels to work
export	sell to other countries
freight	goods carried by trains, ships, planes or trucks
goods	things people buy or sell
port	a place where ships load and unload
rails	the tracks that trains travel on
steam	water changes to this when it is boiled

Index

16